Merle Collins is Grenadian. She has studied at the University of the West Indies, Georgetown University in the United States, and at the London School of Economics and Political Science. Her published work includes a volume of poems, *Because the Dawn Breaks* (1985), a novel, *Angel* (1987), *Watchers and Seekers: Creative Writing by Black Women in Britain* ed. with Rhonda Cobham, 1987, and a volume of short stories, *Rain Darling* (1990). She is currently a lecturer in Caribbean Studies at the Polytechnic of North London. She lives in London.

Rotten Pomerack

Merle Collins

Acknowledgements

The following poems have appeared before in the
publications indicated, by the same author:

'Violence' – an abridged version appeared at the
beginning of *Angel*, The Women's Press, 1987. 'You
Carry My Life', at the beginning of *Rain Darling*, The
Women's Press, 1991. 'how times have changed', and
'Shipmates', *Watchers and Seekers*, Rhonda Cobham &
Merle Collins, The Women's Press, 1987. 'The lesson' and
'Nabel-String', *Because the Dawn Breaks*,
Karia Press, 1985.

Published by VIRAGO PRESS Limited 1992
20–23 Mandela Street, Camden Town, London NW1 0HQ

Copyright © Merle Collins 1992

Printed in Great Britain by Cox & Wyman Ltd,
Reading, Berkshire

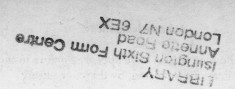
For Keva, my niece

CONTENTS

Remembering yesterday
Longing for tomorrow
while today tiptoes past

IT CROW FIRE

Every so often
on a moonlight night
when something he could only explain
in a story
made him smile
walk high
want to talk in a really intimate
kind of style

my uncle would appear on the top step
with a sasa mi oh!
and a Tim! Tim!
and with a Bashe
the wooden silence would be broken

he would tell the story
not so much from the beginning
as at the beginning

Sese mwen oh!
Sa i ye?
Me father have a cock
when it crow it crow
FIRE

I know!
I know!

You know?
What you know?

A gun!

As it was

in the beginning we knew
but didn't know that we knew

Sese mwen oh!
Sa i ye?

and by now we knew
that the father's cock crowing fire
was really the gun powder's curse
remembered

and knowing that my uncle
could tell the beginning
when the moon made nonsense of reality
people would wait for the light
and walk in its circle

With a Tim Tim
Bois seche

Is who cock that crowing now!
You hear the latest?
Those on the hill selling up
going back to England!

Back?
Is there they come from?

Well
kind of
the great great grandfather

but is not really England, non
is Ireland, yes

England Ireland same thing
Same thing to us out here anyway

So if he goin
What happen to the estate?
Selling up?
Who buying?

Sese mwen oh!
Sa i ye?
Me father have a cock
when it crow it crow . . .

Where your grandpeople from?
No place to go back to?

Come! Come!
Fire me one, non!
Fire me
another one

Children
Tim Tim
Bois seche

Even then we knew the word
but didn't know that we knew
not until later
when uncle
his voice gone quiet
his audience gone
listening elsewhere
the moon no longer lighting
a jagged track through his eyes

lowered his gaze
put his hands in his pockets
turned his seeing from inside
outside
and walked away in search of the place
where real storybook stories are made

Once, years later,
I went to see uncle in a London flat
no step of its own
no space for beginnings
not even for happy remembering

Sese mwen oh!
and my uncle lifted his head
looked at the darkening corner
listened
seemed to see nothing
must have heard nothing
said nothing

But in this darkness
I wanted to hear again
the word that my uncle had known so well
wanted to see the track of the light
in his eyes again
wanted to hear the tone of a story remembered
in his voice again

Sese mwen oh!

but the beginning was gone
my uncle gone silent

After a while
he buttoned the jacket
of his London Underground uniform
picked up his cap
walked towards the darkened doorway
towards the steps
down
to the misty outdoors

turned
found a word
framed a question
in this room in the place
where real storybook stories are made

So you want to hear story now
After one time is two time, yes
Allyou drunk
Allyou joking
Allyou want to know story now.

AT COCK CROW

In the morning
when the cock crowed
the yard was a blaze
of colour

red-skin
fair skin
brown-skin
red red
black black
kind o light-
skinned
not so black
kind of fair skin like
black black
BUT
pretty

near white
with nice nice hair
bad hair
BUT
Indiany like
dougla

and the day they told the dougla
that dougla means bastard
he found no words to respond

until someone explained
that is nobody's fault, really
it's just that in Hindi
there's a word that's dougla
which just happens to mean bastard

and he thought of the word
made man for him

his mother
African black
won't be called African
knows nothing, she says,
of Africa

doesn't like to say black
sounds so kind of harsh
so calls herself coloured instead
wished she needn't think of the coding
the colouring

wanted a light-skinned somebody
just to put a little milk in the coffee
that so bitter when black
just to improve the chances
of the coming generation

and sometimes she remembers
the songs she sang long ago
she remembers the chants
they all chanted

if you white you all right
if you brown, stick around
if you Black,
stand back

When the cock crowed fire
the yard became a blaze of mixed-up
colour.

UP AND DOWN THE DECK

Sea water, they always tell us
from experience
have no branch
so we play our sea-games
on the land
frightened by the sea
haunted by the land

Children
Sea-Water
have no branch, you know

We commandeer a boat
found ourselves a captain
shout
rock the boat
with moving

Up and Down the Deck
Keep Moving
Up and Down the Deck
Keep Moving

Perhaps the past holds us
more tightly than we know
no ship crossing the Atlantic now
The whip-lash is only our chosen captain's voice

but we rush to galley
to quarterdeck
stop to dance
stop to look
stop to listen
for our canny captain's trickery
stop to decide if survival lies
on deck
or overboard

Quarter-deck!
Perhaps it's not the voice
but the hands
that will speak our dying

Up and Down the Deck
Keep Moving!
Up and Down the Deck
Keep Moving!

Boom overhead!
and the yard ducks
swift and silent as death
remembered

Keep Moving
Up and Down the Deck
Up and Down the Deck
and the frenzied song and stomp
begins
again

a story spawned, perhaps, from yesterday
written on pages that do not fade with time
a ship's journal brought to shore
in a children's game of life
and death
remembered

Boom overhead!
sea water
they always tell us
from experience
have no branch

so now
beached on these islands
listening to the sea's thundering whisper
watching its changing waves
we play our frantic sea-games

Up and Down the Deck
Keep Moving
Up and Down the Deck
Keep Moving
Up and Down the Deck
Keep Moving

VIOLENCE

violence comes in gentle form
sometimes
smiling angels, baby Jesus
a perfect virgin mother
sometimes
violence comes in gentle form
the river looks calm until the rain falls
then it vomits old pans, old cans
a tumbling mass of mud
everything swallowed for years gone by
savage indians, heroic pirates
a lazy bumbling Quashee
sometimes
violence comes in gentle form
birdies singing tender little tunes
in some strange season called Spring
coppice gates
where frost is spectre grey
no show of sunshine
no flame-tree
no sea
sometimes
violence comes in gentle form

THE SHEEP AND THE GOATS

this is where you separate the sheep
from the goats

Sometimes
my mother's statements startle
with irrelevance
stay and tickle
disappear to appear again
some unlikely day

Standing in the queue
at the airport terminal
London
Heath-
row

I tried to decide
which were the sheep
and which
the goats

a sudden movement
a twitch
nervous toss of head
to shoulder
a forceful kicking
twitching leg
quick glance through the pages
of a pass-
port
taut tug
at the hand of a fearful child

and
on
the
other
side
the
sheep
serene

a few there
look like us
here
but this is clearly where
you separate
the sheep
from the goats

at the desk
the officer's eyes
proclaim
a cold dislike of goats,
so throats are cleared
for bleating

this is where one begins
to learn
new speaking

when he stamped my pass
I looked down expecting to see
SHEEP

some goats who had tried to wear
sheep's clothing
had been discovered
un-masked
sat silent now along a wall
awaiting return to their pasture

this is where you
separate
the sheep
from the goats

tomorrow
I must write my mother.

SEDUCTION

When first I came wandering
into this cold confinement
My friend talked about things
I couldn't hear then
but listen to now
when voices are louder
with distance brought closer

My Sister, she said
you've come for a year
maybe two
but you'll stay
longer

Life's moving on
patterns are shifting
Times are just changing
And my sister, she said
The longer you linger
in this seductive dying
the more silent, you'll see
You'll become.

Twenty years, she said,
in this cold confinement
and every winter I'm packing
to leave.

Twenty years, she said
putting by a little
for the days that are coming
Not living these days that are going
have gone

Twenty winters
deciding to leave
and stop dreaming
start living
Start hoping again
that times will be changing

Twenty winters
of wanting
to cross the Atlantic
again
to the place of
some kind of homecoming
again

But that's changing
This place is the home of my children
so the picture is shifting
again

Twenty winters of crying to leave
Then summer comes in
gloomy but brighter
life holding some promise again
and I linger
longer
in this seductive dying
this sad and sweet subsisting
and the more silent, it appears,
I become.

Going home becomes harder, she says
cold winter is homely
the fire replaces the sun
and yet there's a longing
for the places that gave me a longing
for leaving

So what keeps me wandering still
she wonders

New roots, she says, new shoots
and home moving further away

my voice becomes weaker
the hope of returning grows fainter
till later when older
when things will be better
but the white clouds are distant and cold
black pride is a promise I keep

and the longer I linger
in this seductive dying
the more silent, my friend,
I feel,
I become.

But perhaps, she says
perhaps there is a foundation
that people like me have been building
perhaps I haven't just wilted
while others have shouted
Perhaps I haven't just wasted and waited
Perhaps my quiet determined surviving
Give shouting voices their strength
Perhaps she says, if I'm not too fanciful
Your shouting, my friend
is only my silence intoned

But sister, I remember,
she pleaded
try not to linger too long
in this seductive dying
this sad and sweet subsisting
or the more silent
you'll see
you'll become.

VISITING YORKSHIRE – AGAIN

Yorkshire was not really as I remembered it
But then, the last time I visited
the Brontës had created for me a world
not so much of Black or white
as of indeterminate shades
of art
that had no colour
of pleasure that existed
for its artistic self

then i loved the cobbled streets
sometimes I even walked
the mystic moors

Yorkshire when I visited, later,
was not exactly as I remembered it
from then

Now people stared at a
Black
woman
walking the cobbled streets
alone
and art, for me
began to have new colour

when I think of their Yorkshire now
I see the cobbled streets
the stark brown of distant trees
the cold silence of shuttered houses
the rolling landscape of the mystic moors
and what one never misses
in England
what one never sees while visiting
with the Brontës, from afar

the glances, the stares
the averted gaze
the quickened step

After the Brontës,
I decided not to visit with Keats
and Wordsworth
Discovered that art
in England
comes in Black and White
in rich and poor
that an art called Black
exists
for England
in some region called the Fringe

Yorkshire was not at all as I remembered it
But then, England is not as I remember it, either,
from the times when my dad smiled and sang
put on his ex-serviceman's uniform
went off whistling to celebrate the day that
WE
had victory in the war.

SHE WAS QUIET

she was quiet
until you looked into her eyes
and then you thought
well, perhaps not so much quiet
as unrevealing

she was meek
moved about the kitchen of her work-place
as if she would step aside
to give an ant the right of way
she was meek

until you looked into her eyes
and then you thought
well, perhaps not so much meek
as undemonstrative

she was mary the cook
who walked without moving
who talked without a voice
who looked without seeing
who listened without hearing

just another faceless person
unseeing and unseen
on the streets of London

not much was ever said of mary
and mary never had much to say
for herself at all
until, one day

you visit the cook in hospital
and she startles you to silence
by meeting your routine how are you

not with well
not with fine
not even with
well, not so well today

but by speaking of her mother
of her son in the village
of Nigeria
and of the world
as if she knew so much
not only of its pain
but also of its possibilities
made impossible

and when Mary's eyes say with searching
how I am is all a part of that
you are silent now
you feel faceless, too

Thank God Mary says thank God
thank God that she had made some time
to visit them in the village last year
her anxious mother and her waiting son

and you had this image of Mary wresting time
from those who had control of it
breaking it like the bottle
and remaking just a little piece
to suit herself, thank God

now they say that if they can find no-one
perhaps they will bury mary
in an unmarked grave
or perhaps they may even cremate mary
and scatter her ashes on a wintry english day

mary who had come to England in search of dreams
who had hoped to go home tomorrow
until the cancer that had been in her life
since yesterday

ate its wary watchful way
into her breast today
and left tomorrow
searching for another day

I wonder who will make some time
who will find the money
that mary never made enough of
here in her English home

to seek and tell her anxious mother
and her waiting son

THE LUMB BANK CHILDREN

Today we walk here where once the miller walked
Imprisoned in time
Confined for a week to the beauty that is now

In the valley the mist hardly ever lifts
the hands that hold that white blanket down
are children's hands, they say
and that wail that wanders nightly
on this December wind
is not a christmas carol
but children howling an ancient hunger
around the mill-house
a gaunt memory of a living graveyard

Last night, while a child's mangled memory
moaned under the misty white
a ghost walked from ancient India's cotton-fields
moved tall and stately through this lonely valley house
connecting

Last night, while wailing carols wandered
in the whitening cold
a figure walked through time and space
from a water-mill somewhere near a Caribbean
cane-field
searching

The restless ghost-child sighed, sucked a thumb,
turned over in her valley bed, and slept.
Early this morning, the mist lifted slowly
And the waterfall shouted a story louder than its voice.

Today we walked where once the miller walked
Released in time
Surrounded for a week by the quiet beauty that is now

YOU CARRY MY LIFE

you carry my life
in the questions in your eyes
in the silence of your fears
in the anguish of your tears

when you let them stop you walking
my step falters
when you let them stop you talking
my voice becomes weaker
when you let them stop you looking
my eyes grow dimmer
when you let them stop you reasoning
my thoughts become confused
if you think they might stop you
wanting to re-create

look for the rest of us
you carry our lives
in the questions in your eyes
just like we carry yours

FOR THE LUMB BANK GROUP,
DECEMBER 1991

Here in this misty valley
you have reminded me of the simple things
that a house is not a home
that warmth may not be a sunny beach
in summer

Here you have been the sand
and I have been the water
You have been the water
And I have been the sand

The cold is still a living force
but you remind me again that
Home is not a house
Happiness is not a heatwave
Warmth might just
sometimes
be found in misty cold.

SHE SITS ON THE TRAIN
AND SINGS INSIDE

She sits on the train and sings inside

Las abété mwen, Naporinden
Las abété mwen
Las abété mwen Naporinden
Las abété mwen
Las abété mwen Naporinden
Las abété mwen

Sits and sings snippets of remembered songs
to keep her feelings company

Oy o yoy! Lord! Look at me crosses!
They want to kill me

she turns her head to the left
and there are two women sleeping
sliding
subsiding
startling and recovering

Oy o yoy! Lord! Look at me crosses!

she looks to the right
a man stands struggling
against the consistent moving
he holds a torch
carries a broom
that must have tried
to sweep the dirty night away

Oy o yoy! Lord! Look at me crosses!

She wonders if the women sleeping
have children too
in St. Kitts
St. Lucia
Jamaica
Grenada

She sits on the train and sings
inside
the songs that keep her thoughts company

Sad to say I'm on my way

She looks
at the three young women opposite
and wonders why they too travel
at 5.15 on this Friday morning
dressed all prim
looking all proper like that
Could they be going to the cinema, too,
to pick up
Bits of paper
Bits of paper
lying on the floor
lying on the floor
they make the place untidy
make the place untidy
pick

The train stops at King's Cross
she watches young people
eyes drunk
or searching
their clothes she can find no
clean words for

In a far corner a man
slumps drunk
sinks dribbling
around him, his life
is scattered
in plastic carrier bags

If London, she wonders,
eats those whom it thinks of as its own
who is me?

Oy o yoy! Lord! Look at me crosses!

the train moves
stops
moves
and the place names sound like books
like dreams
like joy
Covent Garden makes her sit up straight
hold her head high
and yawn
delicately

she looks at the three women opposite
and another song suggests itself

Miss Mary had some fine young lady
fine young lady
fine young lady
Miss Mary had some fine young lady
Tra-la-la-la-la-la

one young woman moves gently on the seat
her back stays straight

and every night is a
sitting on the sofa
sitting on the sofa
sitting on the sofa

Piccadilly Circus is the fun —
place
where she leaves the train
one fine young lady leaves too
so perhaps she goes to the cinema,
after all

Outside, a man is sleeping under Eros
his beard looks like mist
his face looks like death
and Eros, like an angel
points his arrow elsewhere

a woman who last night walked
around the statue
walks still this morning
doesn't seem to want again
to look at any living being
just walks
and mutters to her feet
and walks
around

the fine young lady is walking, too,
towards Leicester Square
perhaps she goes to the theatre

and every night is a
sitting on the sofa

when they pay me this week,
she thinks,
I must put by
ten pounds
to send home
I hope they taking good care of her
I must let them know that
everything is all right
everything okay
and that I working in
Piccadilly Circus
now

back home
the child sits on the sofa
she watches her friends
she fingers a letter
and smiles
she's been reading of places
that sound like books
like dreams
like joy

Me mother in England, yes
she says
and the eyes look at her with envy
Me mother in England
she working in Piccadilly Circus, now,
and she send ten pounds for me

so now with her every night is a
sitting on the sofa
sitting on the sofa
sitting on the sofa
every night is a
sitting on the sofa
tra-la-la-la-la-la

ONE NIGHT

One night I awoke
to the sound of shouts
to running footsteps
I thought the nuclear war had come

What if it had?
What happens in a country
where neighbours can be quite unknown?
Would everyone run to find their shelter?
Would anyone think to call a neighbour?

The night quietened again
The war hadn't come
yet
I must, I thought, find out, some day,
what will happen if it does?

GIFTED

one of the boys giggled and said
he was like a Bounty bar
brown on the outside and
coconut-white inside

like a Bounty bar
because
he's in a school for the gifted
where everyone else is white

he turns over the ruler on his desk
measures the length of the sides
on the blank page on which
he must write

His Mom says
that back where she comes from
there are many who are gifted
and Black
His Mom says
it has nothing to do with
Bounty bars

England, his Mom says,
is full of
a word Dad says he mustn't repeat
but his Mom says why not?

His Mom
says she wants to send him
home
to school
His Dad says
he'll just have to make it
right here
in spite of everything
this is his home, his Dad says
but his Mom says
the sooner he learns that his home
is somewhere else
the better it will be
for him.

His teacher says
his work is not
as good
as it used to be
His Mom says it better be

The boy
turns over the ruler on his
desk
measures the length of the sides
on the page
puts his head down on the desk
and wonders what it's like
that place that his Mom calls
Home

forgets about Bounty bars
lifts his head
listens
thinking of places
where it's ordinary
to be gifted and Black.

CHANT ME A TUNE

When you see me weak and wondering
as you sometimes will
chant me a tune

move with me across the weeping atlantic
through the blood tears death pain and hurt
through the thundering angry sighing sobbing fury
of the startled atlantic
throbbing with the pulsing pages of a story
written as footnotes to an eager quest for land

chant me a tune
move with me beyond the rattle of the chains
and watch me rise with Nanny in Jamaica
where they pulled the cup drained the sorrow
rooted out the pain
and are still seeking beneath the hope

when you see me weak and wondering
as you sometimes will
don't try to dust my story
into the crevices of time
chant me a tune

speak to me of Mary Seacole
who washed their tears
and calmed their fears
and got lost behind white nightingales
somewhere in the telling of their story

when you see me weak and wondering
as you sometimes will
remind me how much
i am a part of your surviving
just as you are a part of my believing

Remind me
that though i am a part of those who died
because they simply could not bear to live
i am also of those who lived
because they refused to die

chant me a tune
speak to me of what we have been
of what we are
of what we are creating

when you see me weak and wondering
as you sometimes will
i need you
to remind me
that, like you,
i am the oceanic roar
of angry strength
that never dies
that never dies
that never will die

WHEN IT'S ALL OVER

when it's all over
while you're regretting its going
don't you wonder sometimes
at its staying
so long?

perhaps he had said well
now show me your motion
and you thought well
okay
tra-la-la-la-la
or in these days when things
don't really follow
the yesterday way
perhaps even the other way round
in the ring
But still
some kind of a
tra-la-la-la-la

all those days of striving
just to keep him wanting
didn't you wonder sometimes about you
perhaps wanting
more than just his judging
perhaps even judging yourself
or were you just lulled
by the consistent chanting
of the tra-la-la-la-la?

And then when you stopped hurting
at his going
and had taken to thinking again
was it then frightening
this no longer caring

this marvel of remembering
the tra-la-la-la-la?

and isn't it frightening
and releasing
this daily discovering
that so much of loving
is more a consequence of
fear of loneliness
than sudden discovery of love?

doesn't it leave you afraid
to keep watching the motion
to keep singing the singing
to keep doing the chanting
of the
tra-la-la-la-la?

Or do you just
do some thinking
some simmering
some shrugging

and end up deciding
Cho!
Tra-la-la-la-la?

HOW TIMES HAVE CHANGED!

I remember how
in days long ago
i would squeeze my eyes tight shut
and pray, tremblingly
Lord, make this relationship work out

even though he's awful
sometimes
you know that truly he's beautiful
inside, Lord
bring out the best in him
make him be really beautiful
Lord, make this relationship work out

and sometimes, I even added
threateningly
or i shall die
and waited for results

perhaps i hoped
that man to man
they'd work it out
and perhaps they did
how times have changed!

now, meeting you,
whom i quite fancy
i say simply
to the watching me
seems to me it would be
quite nice, if something works

if he's beautiful
inside
let him pause
if he's as awful
as i suspect
i'll survive without the hassle

being alone can be quite beautiful
sometimes
loneliness when in company
is a pain i've learnt to fear

how times have changed!
from that
to this
from then
to now
it's funny
and beautifully peaceful
the way times have changed

SOME DAYS, MOTHER

Some days, mother
when my thoughts are a tangle I cannot untie
when meanings are lost and I cannot say why
when the day to day drudging is exhausting not fulfilling
when a hollow space inside says I'm existing not living
Those days, mother
when life is a circle that keeps me spinning not moving

Who else in the world could I tell of the pain?
who else in the world could understand the hurt?
Who else in the world would I simply know is sharing?
who else in the world could so love me in weakness?
Who else, Mother? Who else?

Some days, mother
When the coming of morning is an intrusion I fear
When the falling of night fuels thoughts of despair
When prayer for some deeper believing is a passion
I cannot express
When the tolling of time seems so slow and so pointless

Who else in the world could I tell of the hurt?
Who else in the world wouldn't think me insane?
Who else in the world could love me just for
the sake of loving?
Who else, mother? Who else?

Some days, mother
When I can find no meaning even in your existence
When we quarrel and argue and I wish I never knew
    you
When I listen and look and hope I'm not seeing my
    future
When some other searching has fuelled rejection

Who else in the world would love me again without
    question?
Who else holds this feeling that nothing I do can erase?
Who else is simply always there for my story?
Who else, mother? who else?

Some days, mother,
when I go searching for this kind of loving you're giving
when I go giving this kind of loving you're teaching
It's like trying to hold the rainbow that drinks in the
    river
It's like trying to hug the moonlight that sits on the
doorstep
It's like spinning around in circles and challenging the
    sky
to come falling

So mother, tell me
Who else knows the secret of this deeper loving?
Who else shares the miracle of such tender caring?
Who else is there that knows of this unstinting
    supporting?
Who else, Mother?
Who else?

NEARLY TEN YEARS LATER
(for Grenada)

nearly ten years later
look me here analysing
still distraught and debating
sympathising synthesising
regretting and remembering
and time
just passing

who in the prison frustrating
who done dead disappearing
who alive remonstrating
nuff people still mix up and hesitating
and time
just passing

Grannie used to say
when you ask the question why
child forget that
and then it sound like she
just rambling
child forget that
think bout this

miss nancy etticoat
in a white petticoat
and a yellow nose
the longer she stands
the shorter she grows

Child, you see it?
is the candle
the candle of life
Watch Miss Nancy Etticoat
Look the white petticoat
See the burning nose!

And the white petticoat
Just melting
disappearing
time passing

Child, forget that
think bout this
the shorter she grows
time passing

who in the prison frustrating
who done dead disappearing
who alive remonstrating
nuff people still mix up and hesitating
and time
just passing

like miss nancy etticoat
in she white petticoat
and she yellow nose
the longer she stands
the shorter she grows

time passing

some shouting for hanging
and we wanting an accounting
but watching the children
and dreading more bleeding

the shorter she grows
time passing
the shorter she grows

Like our prophets have asked
who will judge the judges?
child, today for policeman
tomorrow for thief
you see it?
time passing

watch the candle
miss nancy etticoat
and she yellow flame nose
the longer she stands
the shorter she grows

Perhaps the children will judge the judges?
you retreating, they advancing
the shorter she grows

time passing
time passing

UP THE HILL

At home they speak of you
when they do
as
those up the hill

and I think of you
not just some days
but every day
when the sun doesn't shine

I think of you on misty days
on rainy days
on days just hiding in the fog
on those days
when the sun shines
but doesn't burn

I think of you
on the days that I pass
just wanting
not to think of you

on the days when I do not march for you
when I cannot shout for you
when my fist won't
go high for you

and I think of you, too
when I think of words like
petit-bourgeois
like vacillation
like intellectuals

I think of you
when I scratch from a poem the word
anti-imperialist
and seek some more everyday
poetic phrase
when I erase the names of living heroes
and seek safety in tribute to the dead

I think of you
when I think how death
makes saints of sinners

and when I think of death
I think of dreams
buried and speeding and lost
and mostly I think of people
wondering what
and why
and when they talk of killing some
I think of Guatemala
I think of El Salvador
of Chile
and the answers
that people perhaps will never have

and my fist goes
halfway
up
again

asking no questions
I only speak the pain

because I think of you, too
struggling for
your
or was that
our
dream

I think of certainty
I think of shame

and I think, too,
of a quiet, caring, soldier
who understood that dreams had
died
who called me sister
who watched my shaking
who felt my fear
who told me that he, too
was
afraid

I think of you when I write
when I speak
when I think
of writing

I think how
in those days
long, long
before
this hurting
you helped me find
this voice

But then I think of you
dreaming
together
and because you are now alone
together
my belly will only bawl for you
but my fist will not
go high for you

But still
I think of you
on all those days
that I spend just wanting
not to think of you.

NABEL-STRING

The part of me that is there
not here
Home
not wandering
not
chickee baby
not
hey sugar
how you doin, baby?
but
doodoo darling, you alright?

Not going up to this enclosed home
in the elevator
on stairs
in silent
unconcerned
instinctive hostility
with the neighbour I do not know

not turning the key for the umpteenth time
in the door of no. 204 and suddenly pausing
intent
attention on 203
I wonder who living there?

No. not that.
Not that absence of you, of me,
of warmth, of life
but running outside with the piece of bread

Ay! Teacher Clearie!
Shout the bus for me, non!
Ay! Moore, man, you alright?
I tell you already don't smoke that ting, you know

Ay! James! wait! Take the kerosene pan!
I don't taking no damn kerosene pan
Eh! But he ignorant, eh!
Awrite! Awrite!
Bring it!
Ka dammit!

There
where neighbour is friend
and enemy
to be cussed and caressed
so damn annoying you could scream
sometimes
so blasted fast in you business
you could hate
most times

but hate is feeling
loving and cussing and laughing
and needing
is living
that blank stare from the unknown
next door neighbour
kills something inside
makes the warmth inside
bring the tears

and the drum
the drum
the drum that I keep hearing

is River Sallee
is Belmont
is down in the mang
by the cinema dey

You, I, We left
Left to search as always
for a better life
to chase dreams
to find education

Go on, chile, take what I didn't get
you hear
I have nothing left to give
All I have is in you head
Left because every year more out of work
less work to get
because the landless with money
always getting land
and the without money landless
still more landless yet
and still loving
because of a memory

because chemistry in form five this year
and liming on Market Hill straight
for the whole of next year
just didn't kind of make no sense
because love turned hate
is bitter not sweet

and when your cousin the secret police
beat you up and search you
and threaten to report you
you feel like you dying inside
and being reborn of hate
and that hurts

left too because of a need to search
for the reason
the beginning
the end
the all
so left
and will always be leaving

but there's the sound of the heart
beat
of the drum
beat
And me grandmother would always say
Bury the children nabel-string
under the coconut tree, you know
by where I did bury their father own
so the nabel-string, there
and as the palm branch swaying
it pulling
it pulling
it pulling me

back.

A JOURNEY

a journey, perhaps, in search of my soul?
of the power behind my sunday-school self?

God, they told me then
made me
in his own image and likeness.

Almost.

I have the words of the language
they gave me for God's
but the goddess inside changed the music.
I learnt the gestures and movements
they told me were God's
but the goddess inside keeps revolting

and the Goddess grows stronger
Sunday-school voices are fainter
and perhaps this painful dying
this constant questioning
is really a recreation of self

or do i just linger here
as i lingered there
because it's seductive
and i'm seeking an answer
that doesn't exist?

SOON COME

Like I said before
Having a wonder-
full time
Told you also
Will write soon

Well child,
today
soon has come

So let me tell you about this England
and why soon come today

Today someone asked
again
if I write for Black people
Today I smiled
again
at a
Black
face
which alone understands my story here

Today I visited a
Black group
in a Black area
to hear Black history

Child, Soon come today
because it was just one day
too many
of getting through the Blackness
just to Be

Soon come today
because today was
just like

Yesterday
when I watched
a Black film
and the day before
when I saw
a Black play

Soon come today
because this was just
an ordinary day
being
Black
in London

Sister
In this place
so really full of wonder
so many wonders go unseen

A lot more to say
But
this subject makes me tired
So
Good-bye
for now
from your

friend
in London

P.S.:   I went to see Keats' house
          and where the Brontë sisters lived.

P.P.S.: Do you still teach the

          writers
          Milton and Wordsworth?

THE LESSON

You tink was a easy lesson?
Was a deep lesson
a well-taught lesson
a carefully-learnt lesson

I could remember great-grandmammy
brain tired and wandering
mind emptied and filled
bright
retaining
and skilfully twisted
by a sin unequalled by their
Eve's
great-grandmammy
living proof of the power of the word
spoke knowingly of

William the Conqueror
who was the fourth son
of the Duke of Normandy
My Grannie knew that William
married Matilda
that his children were
Robert, Richard, Henry, William and
Adella

Grannie, mind going back
Teaching what she knew
Pick on the boss friend
On the boss hero
William the Conqueror
Grannie didn't remember no
Carib Chief
No Asante king or queen
Her heroes were in Europe

not in the Caribbean
not in Africa

her geography was of the Arctic ocean
and the Mediterranean
she spoke of Novasembla
Francis-Joseph land
and Spitbergen in the Arctic ocean
spoke knowingly of
Corsica, Sardinia
Sicily, Malta
the Lomen Islands
and the islands of the archipelago
in the Mediterranean

Is not no nancy-story, non
is a serious joke
I used to laugh at Grannie
repeat after her
till one day
I check the map
and find
the spelling
little different to how I did think
but the geography straight
like a arrow
tip focusing on the arctic ocean

Then me blood run cold
and me eyes stay fixed
on the arctic circle
watching
Novasembla
and Franz-Josef Land
Watching, lower down,
My Grannie's Faer O'er Islands
in Denmark Strait

Unaccountably feeling the cold grip
of the arctic
noting how
by a cruel trick
my Grannie's mind knew more of this
than of a Caribbean
of an Africa which
did not exist

a wandering planet
spun out of orbit
when for an eternal moment
the world went a little too fast

Teach the slaves
and their children
and their children's children
to know and live for our world
no new creation
just a part of the great everlasting old
arctic and mediterranean

and now we
understanding all of that
and a little more
we will cherish Grannie's memory
but beckon William their conqueror across
to meet and revere our martyrs
and the countries and principles
they fought for

In this beginning
we will rewrite the history books
put William their conqueror on the
back page
make Morgan their pirate
a footnote

Grannies to come
will know of the Arctic Ocean
But will know more of the Caribbean Sea
Of the Atlantic crossing
We will recall with pride our own
So goodbye, William
Good
riddance

Kai sa c'est sa'w
esta es nuestra casa
In whatever language
This is our home.

WHAT TING IS DAT?

what is dis ting
dat they talking bout
each time that I turn?

is a bird? is a bee?
is a thing that does sting?

is a lizard? is a frog?
is a thing that does jump?

you don't mean is a person?
is a being like me?

that could walk? that could talk?
make up me own image an ting?

Then is how come I become a
ethnic minority?

It sound like a germ.
It sound like a worm.
It sound like something
that doesn't quite make the grade

the minority in me mouth
it have a vinegar taste
the ethnic you know
it sounding like nigger to me?
you don't find it sounding
kinda like coolie to you?

Over there in South Africa
Azania to be
It have a few white people
with money that is not really theirs

But we don't usually call them ethnic
Even when is minority
is minority white regime, you know

Down there in the Caribbean
it have a few people that is white
who into surfing and sailing and plant-
ation an ting

With the sun on the skin
and the wind in the hair
Laughter touching the stars
in the coolish night air

But we don't call them ethnic!
We don't even call them minority,
you know

They not non-black
they just positive
alright, okay white

So when you see people dealing
the cards that mark
with their mark

we can't play in the game
as if we in ting
we can't call weself ethnic

We not non-white
we just positive, beautiful
BLACK.

CRICK CRACK

crick!
Crack!
Monkey break he back on a rotten pomerack
crick!
crack!
Monkey break he back on a rotten pomerack

What is the mirage and what reality?
Do we know what is truth and what is truly fiction?

When we were children the signals were clear
somebody say crick we say crack
and we know then was nanci-story time in the place
somebody was going to take a high fall on a slippery lie
so we say look at that eh
Monkey break he back on a rotten pomerack
monkey smash up he back on a rotten pomerack

But what is the mirage and what reality?
Do we know what is truth and what is truly fiction?

crick!
crack!
the little little spider defeat the lion
who thought he was king of the jungle
so we say but look at that!
monkey well smash up he back on a rotten pomerack!

crick!
crack!
you see that ball of fire tumbling down the hill?
pure spirit, you know, even though it looking like it real
monkey mashing up he back on a rotten pomerack!

crick!
crack!
Gentleman that person you walking with
in the long long dress
is really a la diablesse
devil woman with one good foot
and one goat foot

so monkey breaking he back on a rotten pomerack!
But what is the mirage and what reality?
Do we know what is truth and what is truly fiction?

crick!
crack!
come midnight tall tall cake
walking through the streets
all in white icing
Monkey break he back on a rotten pomerack

But some stories come
with no crick with no crack
and still monkey does well
break they back on a
rotten pomerack

no crick no crack
but they go west find India
so just call it West Indies
so we say, well

Look at that!
Not a crick or a crack
But sound like monkey well
breaking he back on some
rotten pomerack

no crick no crack
but 1992 they say
is five hundred years since
the discovery of America

We say
For true? But
look at that!
not a crick or a crack
but monkey well
smashing up he back
on a rotten pomerack

so what is the mirage and
what reality?
do we know what is truth
and what is truly fiction?

in South Africa de klerk
without a krick
without a krack
walking tall tall tall
through the streets
and they say he
freeing the Blacks

I say for true?
Where the blood?
Where the sweat?
Where the tears?
sound like monkey well
breaking he back
on some rotten pomerack

not a krick or a krack
but tall tall cake all in white icing
so what is the mirage and what reality?
Who knows what is truth and what is
truly fiction?

once an African child told me
a story she said she had learnt
at school

slavery, she said,
had been abolished by
a tall, tall, tall white man
in a tall, tall, hat
a man whose name she
couldn't remember

the name had gone
but the image remained
so what is the mirage and
what reality?
do you know what is truth
and what is truly fiction?

until lions have their own historians,
they say,
tales of hunting will always
glorify the hunter

tales of hunting will always
glorify the hunter
until the lioness
is her own
hiss-
-torian

HAVE YOU SEEN THEM?

Have you seen them, too
those exiled men with anxious eyes
who seek relief and perhaps release
in wine, in women, though not so much in song?

Have you, too, seen Africa enraged, enfeebled
Searching on the lonely streets of London?

Have you seen them, too
the women with puzzled eyes
Hoping to find a miracle
Wandering somewhere
in the lonely streets of London?

Have you, too,
picked up a new and shining miracle
and paused to give thanks
that you were not like the rest of them
lost and lonely
in the crowded streets of London?

Have you, too
watched your miracle lose its shine
lost your faith in falling stars
there on the sullied streets of London?

Have you, too
held by day the calm of a steady smile
then closed the door on your smiling face
and watched your mirror with trust to say
Not me
I won't take that dying look
from off the lonely streets of London?

WHEN BRITAIN HAD ITS GREAT

Some people yearn for simple things
Like
Putting the GREAT back into Britain
They cannot hear the strangled haunting voices
of infant sisters
and brothers
who died
because enslaved mothers loved too much
to watch them grow to mate, unloved, unloving
to build GREAT Britain's greatness

Put the GREAT back into Britain
and my GREAT GREAT GREAT grandmother
groans
and churns her graveyard ocean
at the memory of Britain with its GREAT

Put the Great back into Britain
and can't you feel the shivering shake
of a great dead sister
turning to mourn within a canefield grave
dug by Britain with its Great

Put the GREAT back into Britain
and my GREAT GREAT GREAT grandparents'
ghostly hands
touch my face
and ghost faces claim my restless
roving eyes
to whisper

And you
would you, then,
be part of the GREAT British nation, too,
when Britain regains its GREAT?

SCHIZOPHRENIA?

He reached Jamaica in 1760
Left in 1960
Africa was in his face
in the turning of his tongue
but he had learned from Drake
and Hawkins
and all the pirates whom the English loved
to be an English hero
speaking no language Africa called its own
Holding a passport that named him British
He was an English man, he thought

They reached Guyana then British in 1860
Left in 1960
spoke scattered words of Hindi
Had moved, they were told,
from East to West
India
Were British, they could claim

until they moved to Britain
looking for footprints left by their
Longfellows
in the sands of time
and sinking

learning to speak in whispers
learning to shout in silence
learning to search their mirrors
for the faces
the real English saw
learning that Irish was a little less
than English
that Black had
no place at all in British

listening for voices beneath the voices
for the words that weren't spoken

from behind the doors they've closed
in the dummy's voice they use so well
the host ventriloquists wonder
if Blacks are prone
to schizo
phrenia

to this hearing of voices which
some claim
aren't really there

But schizophrenia here
for those who find no
'footprints
on life's solemn main'
is not an illness
but just a way of making sure
of living

WHERE THE SCATTERING BEGAN

Here
where the scattering began
they come to find their faces
again
to measure the rhythm of their paces
against the call of the drum
that talks
against the wail of the piano
that yields music to the thumbs
they come with faces denying their
names gone English
Irish
Scottish
they come with hands that speak
in ways the tongue has forgotten
they come with eyes that tell a story
the brain cannot recall
they come with the blue of the sea so close
that they lift their eyes with yearning
towards the emptiness of the skies
some come with the memory of forest sounds
that they have never known
they come speaking simply of complicated things

Here
hands and eyes and ears
begin to shape answers
to questions
tongue can find no words
for asking

SHIPMATES

I watched him as he entered
i watched how he sat there
hands deep in pockets
face clenched in total black defiance
i watched how his lips relaxed
just barely
when his eyes passed my face
returned
relaxed
wondered if to recognise, perhaps
with cautious smile
moved again
with the easy coldness
born of lifelong practise
born of practical experience
but face not quite so clenched now
for silently he had recognised
another passenger
whose averted eyes
could not possibly mean
offence at errant blackness
and as I recognised and shared his pain
my mind wandered
to his struggles
to his beauty
and loving him
I wondered
wondered so hard
that when I looked up
the giant hand was pulling closed the doors
as the train left my station stop
i wondered
went one stop further

travelled back with clenched faces
black and white
wondered
found no sudden answers
and wandered wondering home

BACK TO THE BEGINNING

When we walked through the castle at
Cape Coast
The guide said

Most of the people taken from here
are supposed to have gone to the
Caribbean

if there really had been a fall
from some place called Eden
the curse for humans
must have been to use words
that could never really give
true meaning

Further along the coast, he said,
is Elmina
from there, people were taken mainly to
Brazil

And we walked
towards the entrance
of the castle at
Cape Coast

There was another party
of another colour
and their guide thought, perhaps,
we might travel together

Our guide looked from them
to us
and shook his head
This trip we would make
alone

through cave dungeons
which, we are told, were packed
where bones were left
where uncovered graves were made
where whispers echo still
where we walk hunched inside
where we stand quiet inside
where we listen
silent
walk
through the darkness
to the gaping hole
beyond

There, for us, there was daylight
with the sea's whispering thunder
below

for them, they said, more darkness
for there the ship waited
with men holding weapons
waiting to crow fire
to keep them moving

Up and Down the Deck
Up and Down the Deck

Is now
as it was
in the beginning

TRUTH AND BEAUTY

i could write about the stars
i could write about the seasons
i could write about
the pale soft light of dawn
tugging at a twanging heart-string

I could write about the evening sun
that whispers to the spirit
of the bright blue sea
and pats to sleep the silver sand

I could write about beauty
beauty that you might say
makes nonsense
of all human search

If i could only shut out
the constant cry of human hunger
the constant laugh of human scorn
the constant wail of humans hurting
the crying shout of human hate
the aching hurt of human pain

if only there were no people
of the kind we know so well
if only there were no people
seeking not just silver sand

but sandy silver, glowing gold
if only there were no people
then we, non-existent, spirits
would be, with absent, colourless
human-kind

we would be the star
we would be the dawn
we would be the sea
and then, perhaps
truth would be perfect beauty

WHEN NIGHT FALLS

When night falls
the women who create
and re-create stories
test the temper of the body

they groan with the pain
of moving
sigh
and declare

Well that is that
the body well tired
Thank the Lord
for another
twenty-four hours

What gone well gone
Tomorrow is another day

When night falls
they bunch their skirts
and sink sighing to the steps

they fan their faces
and assert
that the work was good today

That last load of cane
that last bucket of stone
pull us through
We make it.

they think of the child's teeth
of the school uniform
of the food for the week
they consider the budget
the day just ended

and declare
Well that is that

They test the temper of the body
and decide
Well time to put sleep to bed
Tomorrow is another day

When night falls
they stretch the body
and laugh at its hurting
these women who smile
take time for a little remembering

Child, things good today
Let me tell you bout long time days
You think it was easy?
Let me tell you the story

Laughter massages
the body relaxes
Tongue, teeth and throat
enjoy re-creating

Let me just take
a little rest
they say
these women who weave
the stories

Let me rest first
before going to sleep
Let me rest, child
Tomorrow is another day

The owl hoots
they cross themselves
move eyes to the door
It close? Make sure it close.
Somebody going. I wonder who that?

Close the door
Close the door
It not getting
no soul here tonight

They laugh at their fearing
Stretch
Yawn

Well that is that
Is the day that dying
We see another one through, yes
Thank the Lord

Let sleep go to bed
We'll see what tomorrow will bring
we'll see
what tomorrow will bring.

Other poetry available from Virago

LYRICAL CAMPAIGNS
By June Jordan

'**Whatever her theme or mode, June Jordan continually delineates the conditions of survival – of the body, and mind, and the heart**' – *Adrienne Rich*

One of America's most renowned poets, June Jordan has achieved international acclaim for her virtuoso craft and international concerns. Here we witness the variety and daring of her work – ballads, 'dub' poetry, an unparalleled range of personae and languages, hilarious satire, and witty, precise word choice, rhythm and sound patterning. Her poems address and attack predatory politics and still others offer up elegies for Chile, Guatemala, Palestine. She sings of heroes, heroines, and victims. And she sings of sexual desire and its power. 'Jordan makes us think of Akhmatova, of Neruda. She is among the bravest of us, the most outraged. She feels for all. She is the universal poet.' – *Alice Walker*

THE FAT BLACK WOMAN'S POEMS
By Grace Nichols

'Not only rich music, an easy lyricism, but also grit and earthy honesty, a willingness to be vulnerable and clean'
– *Gwendolyn Brooks*

Grace Nichols gives us images that stare us straight in the eye, images of joy, challenge, accusation. Her 'fat black woman' is brash; rejoices in herself; poses awkward questions to politicians, rulers, suitors, to a white world that still turns its back. In the other sequences of this collection, Grace Nichols writes in a language that is wonderfully vivid yet economical of the pleasures and sadnesses of memory, of loving, of 'the power to be what I am, a woman, charting my own futures'.

Also by Grace Nichols

LAZY THOUGHTS OF A LAZY WOMAN

'Grace Nichols is a talented poet, and her skill with language is most apparent' — *City Limits*

In this sensuous, witty and provocative new collection there are poems of laid-back and not-so-laid-back musings, sagas and spells, thoughts on greasy kitchens and patriarchal theology, bikinis and Caribbean migration. But there are moments of poignancy and loss too — as Grace Nichols takes us through the restless, quirky celebrations of her own imagination.

Born in 1950 in Guyana, where she grew up, Grace Nichols worked as a journalist and reporter. She came to Britain in 1977 and has published several children's books. Her cycle of poems, *i is a long memoried woman*, won the 1983 Commonwealth Poetry Prize.

JUST GIVE ME A COOL DRINK OF WATER 'FORE I DIIIE
By Maya Angelou

'Maya Angelou liberates and exhilarates through her magical, lyrical, mystical medium – poetry' – *Mary Bryce, Tribune*

From this best-selling author comes a marvellous collection of poetry. Poems of love and regret, of racial strife and confrontation, songs of the people and songs of the heart – all are charged with Maya Angelou's zest for life and her rage at injustice. Lyrical, tender poems of longing, wry glances at betrayal and isolation combine with a fierce insight into 'hate and hateful wrath' in an unforgettable picture of the hopes and concerns of one of America's finest contemporary Black writers.

Maya Angelou, writer, dancer, singer, teacher and Black activist, lives in North Carolina. Virago publish *And Still I Rise* and *I Shall Not Be Moved*, as well as the five volumes of her autobiography: *I Know Why the Caged Bird Sings*, *Gather Together in My Name*, *Singin' and Swingin' and Gettin' Merry Like Christmas*, *Heart of a Woman* and *All God's Children Need Travelling Shoes*.

Also by Maya Angelou

AND STILL I RISE

'Maya Angelou writes from the heart and her language rings clear and true . . . Whether joyful, sad or playful, her poems speak with delicacy and depth of feeling' – *Publishers Weekly*

Maya Angelou's poetry – lyrical and dramatic, exuberant and playful – speaks of love, longing, partings; of Saturday night partying, and the smells and sounds of Southern cities; of freedom and shattered dreams. 'The caged bird sings / with a fearful trill / of things unknown / but longed for still / and his tune is heard / on the distant hill / for the caged bird / sings of freedom.' Of her poetry, *Kirkus Reviews* has written, 'It is just as much a part of her autobiography as *I Know Why the Caged Bird Sings, Gather Together in My Name, Singin' and Swingin' and Gettin' Merry Like Christmas*, and *Heart of a Woman*.'

SPRING CLEANING
By Jean 'Binta' Breeze

**'Breeze gives a poetic voice to those who have been silenced
. . . she voices the unquenched anger of black women, from
slavery onwards'** *— Scotsman*

Jean 'Binta' Breeze, acclaimed throughout Britain, Europe
and the Caribbean as poet and performer, offers us a
stunning new collection of poetry. Rich and varied in range,
voice and mood she recalls friends meeting in Kingston
Market ('mout open / story bus out / bwoy / it does soun /
like me and yuh . . . an we whole life / jus jump out / spillover /
and recollect / before we gwaan we ways'), sings of rebellion
and regret, hymns a prayer ('surely goodness and mercy /
shall follow me / she pick up de broom / an she sweeping / all
de days of my life / an she sweeping'), and envisions a new
Caribbean.

This marvellous collection includes one old favourite,
'Riddym Ravings: The Mad Woman's Poem', described by
Mervyn Morris as 'one of the great performance poems in
Caribbean literature'.